Tabitha Program: Workbook

An eight week workshop

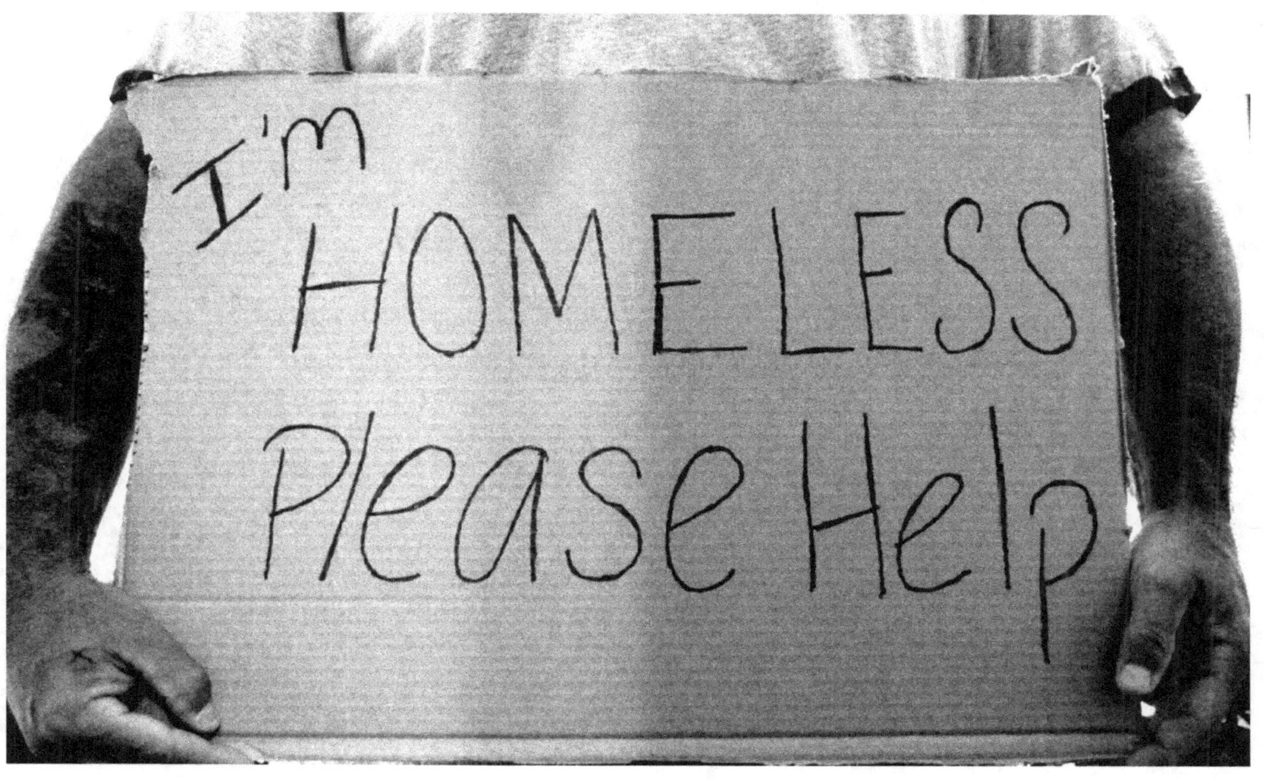

First Edition
2016

Developed by: Bryon Roth

To my wife Barbara who believes in me,
& always inspires me to be a better man.

CONTENT

INTRODUCTION

This workbook is an eight week workshop developed to assist people who are chronically homeless or at risk of becoming chronically homeless overcome obstacles that prevent them from living to their full potential. During the eight week period participants will identify strengths and work to overcome weaknesses. Areas of concentration include past, present and future relationships, goal setting, recognizing stumbling blocks and seeking a better understanding of Spirituality and God.

Along with a personal history, participants will work on a spiritual assessment. The goal of this assessment is to develop spiritually, identifying your own belief system and how that system has affected other areas of your life.

Prior to the first day of this workshop complete the following:

- Read pages 1-3. **Don't** complete the Individual Program Plan (page 6) this is something you will be working on throughout the workshop.
- **Complete** section 1 which is pages 18-30 and make sure you answer each question entirely
- Bring this book with you to the workshop

Human Progress and its Setbacks

Human Growth is a natural response to aging. As we experience life, and endure through difficult times, growth and progress happens. From each heartache and struggle we learn more about ourselves and the world we live in. We develop a conscious understanding of our limits, our strengths, who we are, and what we believe. With every life experience we develop coping skills which help us the next time a similar incident occurs.

Setbacks occur when the normal growth process is interrupted to the extent that it exceeds the individual's internal coping resources. The result can be lasting psychological symptoms. Two major causes of setbacks are childhood neglect and trauma events (to include those witnessed).

"Suffering has been stronger than all other teaching, and has taught me to understand what your heart used to be. I have been bent and broken, but - I hope - into a better shape."
― Charles Dickens, *Great Expectations*

"Out of your vulnerabilities will come your strength."
― Sigmund Freud

Tabitha: A Disciple of Jesus

Acts 9:36-42 - Tabitha Restored to Life

36 Now there was in Joppa a disciple named Tabitha, which, translated, means
Dorcas. She was full of good works and acts of charity. 37 In those days she became ill
and died, and when they had washed her, they laid her in an upper room. 38 Since Lydda
was near Joppa, the disciples, hearing that Peter was there, sent two men to him, urging
him, "Please come to us without delay." 39 So Peter rose and went with them. And when
he arrived, they took him to the upper room. All the widows stood beside him weeping
and showing tunics and other garments that Dorcas made while she was with
them. 40 But Peter put them all outside, and knelt down and prayed; and turning to the
body he said, "Tabitha, arise." And she opened her eyes, and when she saw Peter she
sat up. 41 And he gave her his hand and raised her up. Then calling the saints and
widows, he presented her alive. 42 And it became known throughout all Joppa, and many
believed in the Lord.

The Tabitha Program is geared toward helping men and woman who are either chronically homeless or at risk of becoming chronically homeless. The motivation behind the development of this workbook, and the program, is to help hurting people in Jesus' name.

The word Tabitha is taken from a New Testament disciple whose mission coincides with ours, thus the name Tabitha was adopted in 2012. Scripture indicates she was "A disciple of Jesus", it also states "She was full of good works and acts of charity". Tabitha's love and care for those in need developed from her commitment to Christ as one of His disciples. The fullness of Tabitha's inward grace prompted the outward deeds, or good works. In the same manner the program strives to keep a strong commitment to Christ so that grace may abound.

There are four main components to be implemented with this workbook:

1. Volunteerism: This helps re-establishing work, social habits and self-esteem.
2. Weekly small group meetings: support groups, Bible studies, classes and church attendance, all geared to develop a social network of support.
3. Social outings: to building self-confidence and social skills
4. Completion of an Individual program plan: this helps establish a path to progress, self-sufficiency and permanent housing.

Participant's Commitment

In preparation for the weeks ahead it is important that all participants make a commitment to this workshop.

What is the commitment?

1. To pursue truth in all areas of your life.
2. To make a courageous moral inventory of yourself.
3. To openly and honestly examine you're past to include your beliefs on family, faith, relationships, successes and failures.
4. To complete all assignments in this workbook and actively participate in group and one-on-one discussions.

Commitment to you:

As you enter into this commitment keep in mind it is a relationship between a helper and those being helped.

Helpers Commitment:

1. To provide a safe environment while participants work towards their goals and objectives: Safe physically, mentally and emotionally.
2. To treat participants with Dignity and Respect

INDIVIDUAL PROGRAM PLAN (IPP)

Introduction to IPP

Throughout this workshop participants will develop an Individual Program Plan or IPP. Goals and objectives will be established and areas needing improvement will be identified. The plan will not only help the participant's progress toward permanent housing, but develop strategies geared toward improving their quality of life as well as maintaining permanent housing once achieved. The IPP will identify those factors which resulted in the loss of permanent housing. It will also focus on resources available to help achieve the participant's goals.

Each person's plan is different and unique to them. Areas of concentration include; Housing, Employment, Mental Health, Physical Health, Education, Family, and Spirituality. Participants will begin working on the plan in week two and continue with the facilitators help throughout the workshop. When complete the IPP will be a map to success.

According to the Housing and Urban Development a person is considered 'chronically homeless' when they have been homeless for one full year or they have had four homeless episodes in the last three years. HUD identified four conditions which attribute to chronic homelessness; substance abuse disorder, a serious mental illness, a developmental disability and a chronic physical illness or disability. This program recognizes a fifth condition which attributes to chronic homelessness, the conviction of crimes which are categorized as 'barrier crimes'.

Barrier Crimes – These are barriers to employment and often housing

This is not a complete list

- Felony violation of a protective order
- Murder or manslaughter
- Malicious wounding by mob
- Abduction
- Abduction for immoral purposes
- Assaults and bodily wounding
- Robbery
- Carjacking
- Extortion by threat
- Threats of death or bodily injury
- Felony stalking
- Felony violation of a protective order
- Sexual assault
- Arson
- Drive by shooting
- Pandering
- Crimes against nature involving children
- Incest
- Taking indecent liberties with children
- Abuse and neglect of children
- Failure to secure medical attention for an injured child
- Obscenity offenses
- Possession of child pornography
- Electronic facilitation of pornography
- Abuse and neglect of incapacitated adults

INDIVIDUAL PROGRAM PLAN (IPP)

Name: ______________________________ Date: __________________

Please answer the following questions.

PART I

Place a check mark in any box that applies.

☐ I have a substance abuse disorder.
☐ I have been diagnosed with a mental illness.
☐ I have a developmental disability.
☐ I have a physical illness or disability.
☐ I have been convicted of a barrier crime.

For each box you have checked please explain why you checked that box. Include information such as; mental health diagnosis, physical illness, criminal history, last date you used drugs or alcohol, hospitalization, special accommodations in school, past treatment, time in jail/ prison.

____

____

____

____

____

____

____

____

____

INDIVIDUAL PROGRAM PLAN

PART II – Goals

Goals are the heart of this plan. They represent what you want to do, how you're going to do it, and when you're going to have it completed.

There are six categories:

1. Mental Health
2. Physical Health
3. Education
4. Spirituality
5. Employment
6. Housing

For each of these you will determine if you have issues that need attention or a weakness or barrier that needs to be overcome. You will also identify strengths which will be helpful in completing your goals.

{Example}

Education

Strengths:	**Weakness:**
High School Diploma / College Degree	EMT Certification has expired
Specialized training as an Emergency Medical Tech	

From this exercise I can determine a possible education goal: *Work on getting recertified as an Emergency Medical Technician.*

PART II - Goals

For this exercise you will examine your strengths and weaknesses as they relate to each category. You will then determine what you want to do, which will be your goal.

Remember goals will need to be SMART

1. **S**pecific - Consider who, what, when where, why and how
2. **M**easurable - Include a numeric or descriptive measurement
3. **A**ttainable - Consider the resources needed and set a realistic goal
4. **R**elevant - Make sure the goal is consistent with the mission
5. **T**ime-bound - Set a realistic deadline.

MENTAL HEALTH

Strengths:	Weaknesses:
____________________	____________________
____________________	____________________
____________________	____________________
____________________	____________________

What do you want or need to do (Goal):

____

____

____

PHYSICAL HEALTH

Strengths:	Weaknesses:
____________________	____________________
____________________	____________________
____________________	____________________
____________________	____________________

What do you want or need to do (Goal):

____

____

EDUCATION

Strengths:	Weaknesses:
____________________	____________________
____________________	____________________
____________________	____________________
____________________	____________________

What do you want or need to do (Goal):

____

____

SPIRITUALITY

Strengths:	Weaknesses:
______________________________	______________________________
______________________________	______________________________
______________________________	______________________________
______________________________	______________________________

What do you want or need to do (Goal):

____

____

EMPLOYMENT

Strengths:	Weaknesses:
______________________________	______________________________
______________________________	______________________________
______________________________	______________________________
______________________________	______________________________

What do you want or need to do (Goal):

____

____

HOUSING

Strengths:	Weaknesses:
______________________________	______________________________
______________________________	______________________________
______________________________	______________________________
______________________________	______________________________

What do you want or need to do (Goal):

____

____

PART II - CONTINUED

The next step is to use the goals you have created and put them in the appropriate category on the next two pages. You will also identify specific steps to (objectives) to achieve each goal. Determine a realistic time frame for completion of each step.

INDIVIDUAL PROGRAM PLAN – PART II

	Goal	Steps to Complete Goal	Time Bound
MENTAL HEALTH	________ ________ ________ ________	1. ________ 2. ________ 3. ________	Date: ____ Date: ____ Date: ____
PHYSICAL HEALTH	________ ________ ________ ________	1. ________ 2. ________ 3. ________	Date: ____ Date: ____ Date: ____
EDUCATION	________ ________ ________ ________	1. ________ 2. ________ 3. ________	Date: ____ Date: ____ Date: ____

INDIVIDUAL PROGRAM PLAN – PART II

	Goal	Steps to Complete Goal	Time Bound
Spirituality	____ ____ ____ ____	1. ____ 2. ____ 3. ____	Date: ____ Date: ____ Date: ____
Employment	____ ____ ____ ____	1. ____ 2. ____ 3. ____	Date: ____ Date: ____ Date: ____
Housing	____ ____ ____ ____	1. ____ 2. ____ 3. ____	Date: ____ Date: ____ Date: ____

INDIVIDUAL PROGRAM PLAN – PART II – RESOURCES

	Resource #1	Resource #2	Resource #3	Resource #4	Resource #5
Mental Health					
Physical Health					
Education					
Spirituality					
Employment					
Housing					

INDIVIDUAL PROGRAM PLAN

PART III

Social Network

Your social network will be made up of people who agree to hold you accountable to a commitment of change and progress.

- ✓ I will locate and attend a local church, not just as a spectator but as an active participant.
- ✓ I will attend one community activity, other than Sunday Worship, at my church.
- ✓ I will read the Bible and pray daily.
- ✓ I will participate weekly in an event where I can be in community with other people so I can grow a community of support.
- ✓ I will attend social gatherings and outings, and help with these activities when needed.
- ✓ I will willingly volunteer my time for the benefit of my community to enhance my skills, gain new experiences, and sustain my work ethic and increase my feelings of self-worth.
- ✓ I will be a model for others by developing good spending and savings habits.
- ✓ I will strive to live healthy, working toward good physical and mental health.
- ✓ I will live transparently, asking others to support, encourage and hold me accountable to the commitments I make today.
- ✓ I will support, encourage and hold accountable my brother and sister program participants to the commitments we have made to this Program

____ ____________________

Signature Date

The people signing this letter for me agree to be in relationship with me and be mutually accountable with me to the commitments above.

	Printed Name:	Signature:	Telephone:
*Church			
*Outside Group			
*Program			
Family			

***Note**: Your ministerial staff may not sign for you; it must be others from your church and social group. More than 2 may sign, but 2 are required for each category.

I verify that the above named people have met together to discuss their role in holding the participant accountable.

Facilitator's Signature____

SECTION 1

Exercise: Biographical Data

Name ____ Age ______________

Date of Birth ____

Place of birth ____

Where do You Consider Home ____

Race/Ethnic Designation ____

Relational/Marital Status____

Emergency Contact:

____________	____________	____________	____________
Name	Phone	Address	Relationship

If presently married, date of marriage ________________ Spouse's first name __________

If widowed, divorced, or remarried, please give date(s) when previous marriage(s) began and ended.

____

If you have children, list them by first name, date of birth, and gender.

Name	Date of Birth	Gender	Where They Live	Last Visit

List members of your family of origin, (F) father, (M) mother, (S) sister, (B) brother, chronologically, beginning with the oldest. If any are deceased, place (D) after the age at the time of death.

F, M, S, B, Sf	Name	Age	City/ State	Relationship: (Good, Bad, None)

Are you currently involved in a romantic relationship? ☐ Yes ☐ No

If yes, describe your relationship with your significant other: ______________________________

____

What were the circumstances leading up to being homeless? (be specific, give dates)?

____

____

____

____

____

____

____

____

____

____

____

____

____

____

____

____

____

____

____

____

____

____

Residential History

List the residents/ group homes in which you have lived from birth to present. Give the years, your ages, and the names of the household members. Under "Comment" you may add an explanation, such as "in foster home," or you may wish to comment on how you felt about living in each location.

Dates	Age(s)	Address	Household Members	Comment

"We are products of our past, but we don't have to be prisoners of it."

– Rick Warren

Work History

List all major job experiences and/or significant volunteer services since high school, include dates, employer, and type of position. For each, indicate *overall level of satisfaction* from **1 *(very low)* to 6 *(very high).*** Also, comment in a few words on what was most and/or least satisfying about the work.

Dates	Employer	Position	Salary	Satisfaction Level	Comments

Education History

List all schools you attended

Dates	School	City/ State	Graduated – Yes, No

(Circle one)
Do you have a Learning Disability? YES NO

If yes, Explain ____

____

____

Did you attend special classes in school? YES, NO

Military History

Have you ever been in the military? YES, NO If Yes, dates of service: ______________

Type of discharge: ______________ Do you have military benefits: ______________

Do you have your DD214: YES, NO

Where were you stationed: ____

Why did you leave the military: ____

____

Medical History

Height: _____ Weight: _____ Date and year of last physical: _______________

Are you currently over or under weight? ❑ Yes ❑ No (+) _____ (-) _____

Have you ever had control problems with food? ❑ Yes ❑ No

If yes, explain: ____

____

____

Have you ever had convulsions or seizures: ❑ Yes ❑ No

Are you currently taking any medications? ❑ Yes ❑ No

If yes, what medications are you taking and what are they for?

____

____

____

Do you have any allergies to penicillin, other antibiotics, aspirin, codeine, morphine, bee stings, or any other drugs or food, etc.? If yes, what? Please list:

____

____

Date of last TB test: ______________ Results: ❑ Positive ❑ Negative

Date of last AIDS test: __________________ Results: ❑ Positive ❑ Negative

General Medical Symptoms

- ❑ Trouble Sleeping
- ❑ Loss of appetite
- ❑ Eye / vision problems
- ❑ Frequent headaches / pains
- ❑ Allergies
- ❑ Blood in stool
- ❑ Tremors
- ❑ Convulsions or seizures
- ❑ Persistent cough / cold
- ❑ Difficulty breathing
- ❑ Vomiting
- ❑ Sores that don't heal
- ❑ Venereal disease
- ❑ Hepatitis: Type _____

  When _____
- ❑ Suicide attempts
- ❑ Other: _______________
- ❑ Rapid weight gain / loss
- ❑ Diarrhea / constipation
- ❑ Sexual problems
- ❑ Stomach problems / ulcers
- ❑ Liver problems
- ❑ Diabetes
- ❑ Coughing up blood
- ❑ High blood pressure
- ❑ Hypoglycemia
- ❑ Pancreatitis
- ❑ Contagious condition
- ❑ Gastritis
- ❑ Thyroid Problems

Are you currently under the care of any of the following?

- ❑ Physician
- ❑ Psychiatrist
- ❑ Psychologist
- ❑ Therapist

If so, may we contact them? ❑ Yes ❑ No

Name: ______________________________ Phone: ____________________

Name: ______________________________ Phone: ____________________

What are your diagnoses? ____

____

Psychiatric / Psychological Conditions

Describe any family history of mental illness, alcohol / drug abuse, etc.: ____________

____

____

____

Have you ever been diagnosed with a psychological condition? Please list: __________

____

____

Have you ever been hospitalized for mental health or psychiatric problems? Please list:

Date	Hospital	Reason
_______	____________________	____________________________
_______	____________________	____________________________
_______	____________________	____________________________

Legal Status

Are you currently involved in any of the following legal matters? ❑ Yes ❑ No

❑ Probation ❑ Parole
❑ Divorce Proceedings ❑ Civil Proceedings
❑ Child Care Custody ❑ Drinking Driver Program
❑ Assault charges

Do you have a court appearance pending? ❑ Yes ❑ No

If yes, when and where? ____

How much time have you spent in: Prison ____________ Jail: ____________

List all prior convictions:

Conviction	Date(s)	Time Served

Probation Officer's Name: ____

Telephone: ____

How often do you have to report? ____

TRAUMA HISTORY QUESTIONNAIRE

The trauma history questionnaire is a series of questions about serious or traumatic life events. These types of events occur with some regularity, although we would like to believe they are rare, and they affect how people feel about, react to, and/or think about things subsequently. The questionnaire is divided into questions covering crime experiences, general disaster and trauma questions, and questions about physical and sexual experiences.

For each event, please indicate (circle) whether it happened and, if it did, the number of times and your approximate age when it happened (give your best guess if you are not sure). Also note the nature of your relationship to the person involved and the specific nature of the event, if appropriate (Green, 1996).

	Crime-Related Events	**Circle one**		***If you circled yes, please indicate***	
				Number of times	**Approximate age(s)**
1	Has anyone ever tried to take something directly from you by using force or the threat of force, such as a stick-up or mugging?	No	Yes		
2	Has anyone ever attempted to rob you or actually robbed you (i.e., stolen your personal belongings)?	No	Yes		
3	Has anyone ever attempted to or succeeded in breaking into your home when you were <u>not</u> there?	No	Yes		
4	Has anyone ever attempted to or succeed in breaking into your home while you <u>were</u> there?	No	Yes		
	General Disaster and Trauma	**Circle one**		***If you circled yes, please indicate***	
				Number of times	**Approximate age(s)**
5	Have you ever had a serious accident at work, in a car, or somewhere else? (**<u>If yes</u>**, please specify below) ______________________________	No	Yes		
6	Have you ever experienced a natural disaster such as a tornado, hurricane, flood or major earthquake, etc., where you felt you or your loved ones were in danger of death or injury? (**<u>If yes</u>**, please specify below) ______________________________	No	Yes		
7	Have you ever experienced a "man-made" disaster such as a train crash, building collapse, bank robbery, fire, etc., where you felt you or your loved ones were in danger of death or injury? (**<u>If yes</u>**, please specify below) ______________________________	No	Yes		

8	Have you ever been exposed to dangerous chemicals or radioactivity that might threaten your health?	No	Yes		
9	Have you ever been in any other situation in which you were seriously injured? (**If yes**, please specify below) ______________________________	No	Yes		
10	Have you ever been in any other situation in which you feared you might be killed or seriously injured? (**If yes**, please specify below) ______________________________	No	Yes		
11	Have you ever seen someone seriously injured or killed? (**If yes**, please specify who below) ______________________________	No	Yes		
12	Have you ever seen dead bodies (other than at a funeral) or had to handle dead bodies for any reason? (**If yes**, please specify below) ______________________________	No	Yes		
13	Have you ever had a close friend or family member murdered, or killed by a drunk driver? (**If yes**, please specify relationship [e.g., mother, grandson, etc.] below) ______________________________	No	Yes		
14	Have you ever had a spouse, romantic partner, or child die? (**If yes**, please specify relationship below) ______________________________	No	Yes		
15	Have you ever had a serious or life-threatening illness? (**If yes**, please specify below) ______________________________	No	Yes		
16	Have you ever received news of a serious injury, life-threatening illness, or unexpected death of someone close to you? (**If yes**, please indicate below) ______________________________	No	Yes		
17	Have you ever had to engage in combat while in military service in an official or unofficial war zone? (**If yes**, please indicate where below) ______________________________	No	Yes		

	Physical and Sexual Experiences	Circle one		*If you circled yes, please indicate*	
				Repeated?	Approximate age(s) and frequency
18	Has anyone ever made you have intercourse or oral or anal sex against your will? (**If yes**, please indicate nature of relationship with person [e.g., stranger, friend, relative, parent, sibling] below) ____________________	No	Yes		
19	Has anyone ever touched private parts of your body, or made you touch theirs, under force or threat? (**If yes**, please indicate nature of relationship with person [e.g., stranger, friend, relative, parent, sibling] below) ____________________	No	Yes		
20	Other than incidents mentioned in Questions 18 and 19, have there been any other situations in which another person tried to force you to have an unwanted sexual contact?	No	Yes		
21	Has anyone, including family members or friends, ever attacked you with a gun, knife, or some other weapon?	No	Yes		
22	Has anyone, including family members or friends, ever attacked you without a weapon and seriously injured you?	No	Yes		
23	Has anyone in your family ever beaten, spanked, or pushed you hard enough to cause injury?	No	Yes		
24	Have you experienced any other extraordinarily stressful situation or event that is not covered above? (**If yes**, please specify below) ____________________	No	Yes		

Reference:

Green, B. L. (1996). Trauma History Questionnaire. MD: Sidran Press.

SECTION 2

Exercise: Goal & Objectives

What are goals and objectives?

Goals are general guidelines that explain what you want to achieve in your life. They are usually long-term and represent an overall vision such as "get a job or get your own house."

Objectives define strategies or implementation steps to achieve the identified goals. Unlike goals, objectives are specific, measurable, and have a defined completion date. They are more specific and outline the "who, what, when, where, and how" of reaching the goals.

Why set goals?
Having a written goal along with steps to reach that goal gives you something to plan and work towards. It also lets you visualize and mentally picture how the goal will be accomplished. A written goal is an external representation of your inner desires; it's a constant reminder of what you need to accomplish.

A common acronym used when developing goals is "SMART"

When you set a goal make sure it is SMART:

- **Specific** - consider who, what, when where, why and how in developing the goal
- **Measurable** - include a numeric or descriptive measurement
- **Attainable** - consider the resources needed and set a realistic goal
- **Relevant** - make sure the goal is consistent with the mission
- **Time-bound** - set a realistic deadline.

Goal Review:

What is one goal from your past which you successfully achieved? ______________________

____

____

How long did it take you to reach that goal? ______________________________________

What were some objectives (or steps) you had to complete to reach this goal?

____

____

____

Looking back, is there anything you would have done differently to achieve this goal?

____

____

____

How did reaching this goal affect your life? ______________________________________

____

____

____

____

How did completing this goal make you feel? ____________________________________

____

My Goals

There are probably many goals you would like to achieve in your life; some might be from past failures, broken relationships or dreams you have had for years. Today you need to prioritize the vision you have for your life into needs and wants. What is your immediate need? If you are homeless you have a need for financial stability and then a goal for housing. Remember goals need to be "SMART". Determine what the priority is for your life today and set that as your first goal.

Goal#1: ____

What steps need to be taken to reach this goal? Remember, these are the actions to be taken in order to reach this goal.

List objectives to completing this goal (be specific)	Date step will be completed
____________________________________	______________________________
____________________________________	______________________________
____________________________________	______________________________
____________________________________	______________________________
____________________________________	______________________________

What obstacles might hinder you from completing this goal?

____

____

How can you overcome these obstacles?

____

____

____

____

Who will hold you accountable to completing your objectives? ________________

What are resources you can use to complete this goal?

____

____

____

____

____

How does completing this goal help you now? ______________________

____

____

____

____

____

Social Goal

Your second goal is going to be a social goal and will relate to relationships. This goal can be to reconnect a broken relationship or develop new relationships (non-romantic). This would include purposely working on a friendship with someone at church, work or joining a small group to include; clubs, faith based groups, parks and rec classes/ sporting activities, etc.

Goal#2: ____

What steps need to be taken to reach this goal? Remember, these are the actions to be taken in order to reach this goal.

List objectives to completing this goal (be specific)	Date step will be completed
____________________	____________________
____________________	____________________
____________________	____________________
____________________	____________________
____________________	____________________

List any obstacles you can think of which may hinder completing goal.

____

____

____

How can you overcome these obstacles?

____

____

____

____

Who will hold you accountable to completing your objectives? ______________________________

What are resources you can use to complete this goal?

____

____

____

____

____

How does completing this goal help you now? ____

____

____

____

____

____

Applying what you've learned

What have you learned from this exercise? ____

____

____

____

____

____

____

How will you apply what you've learned in this exercise to your life (be specific)? ____________

____

____

____

____

____

____

____

____

____

How will your life be different by applying what you've learned and achieving your goals (be specific)? ____

____

____

____

____

____

"Anything Your Mind Can Conceive & Believe YOU Can Achieve". ~N Hill

---

SECTION 3

Spirituality

Exercise: Spirituality

What is Spirituality? Spirituality has been defined in numerous ways. This includes: a belief in a power operating in the universe that is greater than oneself, a sense of interconnectedness with all living creatures, and an awareness of the purpose and meaning of life and the development of personal absolute values. It's the way you find meaning, hope, comfort, and inner peace in your life

Good Spirituality. . .

- Relieves stress.
- Helps to improve health.
- Results in less fear of death.
- Gives purpose to everyday life.
- Helps an individual appreciate life and the beauty in the world.
- Helps with forgiveness.
- Facilitates love and trust.
- Helps prevent depression.

Spirituality can also have a negative effect when it is not well defined, miss-interpreted, or creates unrealistic expectations. Developing a healthy understanding of spirituality and defining your own beliefs will help enrich your mental state. Debunking myths or false ideas will help clear your mind and help provide the peace and empowerment available through spirituality.

Spiritual Assessment

What does "spirituality" mean to you? ____

____

(Circle one)
Do you believe in God? YES NO

What if any is your religious affiliation? *(Christian, Muslim, Jehovah Witness, etc.)* ______________

Have there been changes to your religious affiliation over time? YES NO

If yes, please explain, ____

____

____

Level of present involvement in faith-based community - scale: 1-5 (1 = very little, 5= very active)

Circle one:

1 2 3 4 5

Who from your past exemplifies what you think a spiritual person should be like? __________

What character traits did this person demonstrate?

____

____

____

____

In three words or less, what thought or feeling comes to mind when you think of this person?

____

What is you earliest memory of spirituality, religion or God? This may be your first memory or thoughts of religious ideas or an event.

____

____

____

____

____

____

____

____

____

____

____

____

____

How do you think God sees you? ______________________________________

____

____

____

What is sin?

Does God forgive evil or sin? Explain

Do you believe God takes an interest in your life? If yes, to what extent? ____________________

____

____

____

____

____

____

____

Is there life after death? Please explain your reasoning behind your answer. _________________

____

____

____

____

____

____

____

Has there been a spiritual experience which has changed or greatly impacted your life? Explain.

____

____

____

____

Christianity

What is a Christian? ____

What is the Bible? ____

____

____

Who is the Jesus? ____

____

____

How are Christians forgiven of their sins? ___________________________

____

____

How does a Christian get to heaven? _______________________________

____

____

What is your impression of Christianity or Christians? ________________

____

____

Do you feel comfortable in a Christian Church? YES NO

What do you like about Christianity?

____

____

____

____

____

What do you dislike about Christianity?

____

____

____

____

How did you learn about Christianity?

____

____

____

____

____

Did someone take you to Church when you were young? Yes No

If yes, who was that person? ______________________________

SECTION 4

Exercise: Relationships

We were made to be in relationships. Healthy relationships help create healthy lives. From your past you can identify relationships which had a positive impact on your life as well as those which had a negative and possibly even a crippling effect on your life. It is the negative relationships which build walls and prevent you from developing new healthy relationships.

In order to understand relationships, it is important to be able to identify characteristics of both healthy and unhealthy relationships.

Healthy vs. Unhealthy Relationships

Healthy	**Unhealthy**
Supportive	name calling—fat, ugly, stupid
Good communication	controlling
Trust	hates your friends & family
Honesty	cheating
Friendly	needy—dependent
Loyal	lying
Accepting	rude
Compatibility	disrespectful
Respectful	jealous
Equality	neglect
Affection	verbal abuse
Understanding	nothing in common
Space	physical abuse
Kindness	Jealousy
Physical attraction	

From the 'Healthy' list above list the 5 character traits that are most important to you in a relationship.

1. ______________________________
2. ______________________________
3. ______________________________
4. ______________________________
5. ______________________________

Do You Make A Good Friend?

Past Relationships

As you recall past relationships, specific people will be identified by either healthy or unhealthy character traits. In reviewing the list above can you can identify past friendships/ relationships which would fall into each of the listed categories. Recognizing a friendship that had more of the unhealthy characteristics will help you understand why the relationship failed or why it left you feeling empty.

Identifying relationships which had more healthy characteristics will help you understand why that relationship thrived. Those healthy relationships are also the ones we miss and seek to imitate.

Point to Ponder

Just because a relationship experiences some of the unhealthy characteristics from time to time doesn't make it unhealthy as a whole. People make mistakes and sometimes lack of communication or misconceptions lead people to raise their defenses to prevent themselves from getting hurt. When doing so those defenses can oftentimes be perceived as an unhealthy characteristic (ex. Rude, disrespectful, jealous, neglect).

(Circle one)

1. Can you recall a relationship which you now identify as unhealthy? YES NO

2. List 2 characteristics which identify that relationship as unhealthy.

____

____

3. How did that relationship make you feel? ____

____

There is a saying that the past predicts the future. In a lot of ways that is true but it doesn't have to remain true. Understanding how past events affected you and your thinking will help overcome false ideas developed as a means for protecting yourself.

4. How have past unhealthy relationships affected you today when it comes to making new friends?

____

____

____

5. Do you consider yourself a good friend to people? Yes No

6. What makes you a good friend?

____

____

7. Do you let people get close to you? Yes, No If no, explain_______________________________

____

____

8. Do you currently have a close relationship/ friendship? YES NO

9. How can you avoid unhealthy relationships today? ____________________________________

____

____

10. Describe your ideal future in regard to relationships (friendship, marriage, children, activities, etc.)

____

____

____

____

____

____

____

____

____

Childhood Family/ Guardian History

Although there are many commonalties, everyone's experience of family is different. Generally, what is learned in the family during childhood profoundly influences one's adult lifestyle and vocation. The following questions are designed to help understand the nature of that influence in your life. ***Respond to them in terms of your experience from birth to approximately age 18.***

Who were the *three* people most significant to you in your experience of family? Identify them and for each give three words to describe them. This could have been healthy or unhealthy.

Name:______________________________

Three descriptive words __________________, ___________________, __________________

Name:______________________________

Three descriptive words __________________, ___________________, __________________

Name:______________________________

Three descriptive words __________________, ___________________, __________________

For each of the three persons above, describe your relationship growing up.

Family Member #1_______________________________

Was this a healthy or unhealthy relationship? ___________________________

What did you appreciate about this person?

____

____

____

What effect did their life have on your thinking about yourself?

____

____

____

____

____

What effect did their life have on your thinking about education?

____

____

____

____

What effect did their life have on your thinking about family?

____

____

____

____

What effect did their life have on your thinking about faith?

____

____

____

____

Did this relationship help you or hinder you? Please explain. ____________________________

____

____

____

____

____

____

____

Family Member #2 _________________________________

Was this a healthy or unhealthy relationship? _____________________________

What did you appreciate about each this person?

____

____

____

What effect did their life have on your thinking about yourself?

____

____

____

____

____

What effect did their life have on your thinking about education?

____

____

____

____

What effect did their life have on your thinking about family?

____

____

____

____

What effect did their life have on your thinking about faith?

____

____

____

____

Did this relationship help you or hinder you? Please explain. ____________________

____

____

____

____

____

Family Member #3 ______________________________

Was this a healthy or unhealthy relationship: ___________________________

What did you appreciate about each this person?

____

____

____

What effect did their life have on your thinking about yourself?

____

____

____

____

____

What effect did their life have on your thinking about education?

____

____

____

____

What effect did their life have on your thinking about family?

____

____

____

What effect did their life have on your thinking about faith?

____

____

____

____

Did this relationship help you or hinder you? Please explain. _______________

____

____

____

____

____

____

____

Applying What You've Learned

What have you learned from this exercise? _______________________

____

____

____

____

____

____

How will you apply what you've learned in this exercise to your life (be specific)? ____________

____

____

____

____

____

____

____

____

____

From healthy relationships we can develop a lot of positive healthy traits to include a healthy self-image. Relationships which were unhealthy (including those which were abusive) can result in years of pain, grief and negative self-image. Examining these relationships can be a good healthy first step toward healing.

•

SECTION 5

Exercise: Identifying Stumbling Blocks

Stumbling blocks refer to an obstacle or hindrance to progress. They can be internal or external. An example of an external stumbling block might be past debt or a criminal record. Examples of internal stumbling blocks include; bitterness, rebellion, pride, or self-defeat.

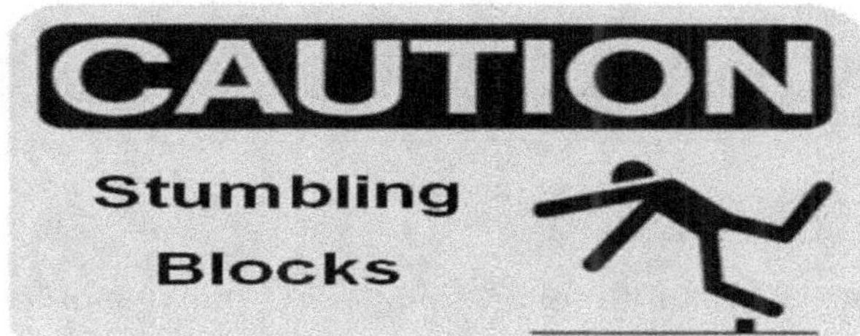

Those stumbling blocks listed as internal can be overcome. Most are related to your perception, or how you see the world around you. They are developed by past experiences and are tied into your thought process and beliefs. External stumbling blocks are often out of your control and require a response plan. A past criminal history can't be changed however, recognizing the limitations and identifying possible avenues for progress will empower you to move past this stumbling block.

REMEMBER: *"I can do all things through Christ who strengthens me."*
~Philippians 4:13

Example of external stumbling blocks:

- Past Debt
- Criminal Record
- Failed Relationships
- Education Failures
- No Transportation
- No Medical Insurance
- Failing Health

External Stumbling Block:

List what you would consider to be your external stumbling blocks.

1. ______________________________________

2. ______________________________________

3. ______________________________________

For each stumbling block explain your reasoning for adding it to this list.

<u>Stumbling block 1</u>

What makes this a stumbling block? ____

____

____

How does this restrict your progress? ____

____

____

____

How can you overcome this stumbling block, what needs to be done to progress? __________

____

____

____

____

Stumbling block 2

What makes this a stumbling block? ____

____

____

How does this restrict your progress? ____

____

____

____

How can you overcome this stumbling block, what needs to be done to progress? __________

____

____

____

Stumbling block 3

What makes this a stumbling block? ____

____

____

How does this restrict your progress? ____

____

____

____

How can you overcome this stumbling block, what needs to be done to progress? __________

____

____

____

____

Internal Stumbling Block – Your thoughts and behaviors that get in the way of your growth progress.

Examples of internal stumbling blocks:

- Bitterness
- Rebellion
- Pride
- Self-defeat
- Boredom
- Frustration
- Inflexibility
- Too comfortable
- Fear
- Focusing on the Negative

List what you would consider your internal stumbling blocks.

1. ________________________________

2. ________________________________

3. ________________________________

For each stumbling block explain your reasoning for adding it to this list.

Stumbling block 1

What makes this a stumbling block? ____

____

____

How does this restrict your progress? ____

____

____

____

How can you overcome this stumbling block, what needs to be done to progress? _________

____

____

Stumbling block 2

What makes this a stumbling block? ____

____

____

How does this restrict your progress? ____

____

____

____

How can you overcome this stumbling block, what needs to be done to progress? __________

____

____

____

____

Stumbling block 3

What makes this a stumbling block? ____

____

____

How does this restrict your progress? ____

____

____

How can you overcome this stumbling block, what needs to be done to progress? __________

____

____

____

Applying What You've Learned

What have you learned from this exercise? ____

____

____

____

____

____

____

How will you apply what you've learned in this exercise to your life (be specific)? ____________

____

____

____

____

____

____

SECTION 6

Exercise: Exploring the Bible

Many people go to church all their lives without knowing why they believe, what they believe. The last three sections in this workshop will focus on developing a better understanding of spirituality and Christianity. The exercises will assist you in either building or strengthening your own spiritual self. As you seek to understand Christianity there are two principles to keep in mind. First, Christianity is based on the teachings of Jesus Christ and the understanding that Jesus is God. Second, the Holy Bible is considered God's word and the source Christians use to understand God.

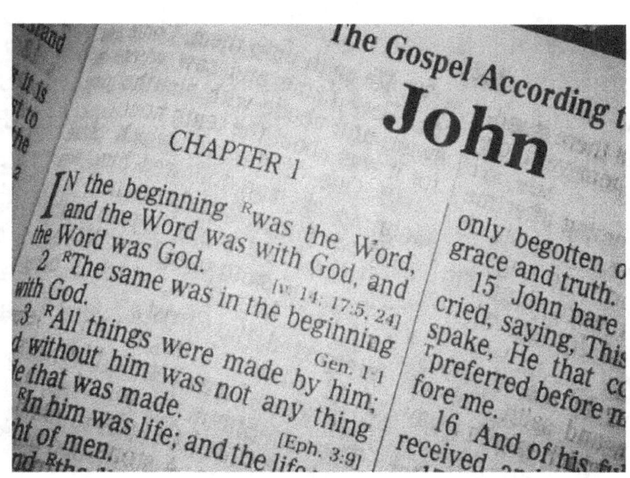

About the Bible

The Bible is the number one source of information for Christians. The Bible teaches about God, Jesus, salvation and everything a Christian needs to know about the Christian life. The Bible contains 66 books, divided among the Old and New Testaments.

<u>**The Old Testament is made up of 39 books**</u>

Pentateuch - 5 books
Genesis, Exodus, Leviticus, Numbers, Deuteronomy

Historical Books - 12 books
Joshua, Judges, Ruth, First Samuel, Second Samuel, First Kings, Second Kings, First Chronicles, Second Chronicles, Ezra, Nehemiah, Esther

Poetic books - 5 books
Job, Psalms, Proverbs, Ecclesiastes, Song of Solomon

Prophetic books - 17 books
<u>*Major Prophets*</u> - Isaiah, Jeremiah, Lamentations, Ezekiel, Daniel
<u>*Minor Prophets*</u> - Hosea, Joel, Amos, Obadiah, Jonah, Micah, Nahum, Habakkuk, Zephaniah, Haggai, Zechariah, Malachi

<u>**The New Testament is made up of 27 books**</u>

Historical Books - Matthew, Mark, Luke, John, Acts

Pauline Epistles (letters) Romans, 1 Corinthians, 2 Corinthians, Galatians, Ephesians, Philippians, Colossians, 1 Thessalonians, 2 Thessalonians, 1 Timothy, 2 Timothy, Titus, Philemon

Non-Pauline Epistles (letters) Hebrews, James, 1 Peter, 2 Peter, 1 John, 2 John, 3 John, Jude, Revelation

Bible Exercise

> *"All Scripture is inspired by God and profitable for teaching, for reproof, for correction, for training in righteousness; that the man of God may be adequately, equipped for every good work," (2 Tim. 3:16).*

In the following exercise's you will need a Bible. A helpful companion to the Bible is a concordance. A concordance is an alphabetical index of the principal words found in the Bible with their immediate context (Usually found in the back of a Bible). This can be helpful to look up subject matter by key words.

The goal of this exercise is to examine Scripture for yourself and determine what the Bible says and how you interpret the scripture. You will be asked a series of questions. For each question multiple passages will be provided. Lookup and read each one to determine which ones best answers the questions being asked. It is often necessary to read the key verse given and several verses before and after the key verse to get a good understanding of what is being said. For each question choose three separate scriptures which answer the question. Make sure you read all verses provided before choosing which ones you will use.

1. What does the Bible say about seeking God?

(Read all of the provided scripture before determining which passages answer this question)

Luke 6:31, Mark 12:31, Jeremiah 29:12-14, Proverbs 3: 5-6 , Deuteronomy 4:29, Psalm 119:10–17, Proverbs 8:17, Hebrews 11:6, Matthew 7:7

Scripture: ____________________________

Paraphrase (In your own words) ____

____

____

Please explain what this scripture means to you. _______________________________________

____

____

____

Scripture: ______________________________

Paraphrase (In your own words) ____

____

____

Please explain what this scripture means to you. ____

____

____

Scripture: ______________________________

Paraphrase (In your own words) ____

____

____

Please explain what this scripture means to you. ____

____

____

____

Based on the scripture you just found in the Bible and your own interpretation, what do you believe the Bible teaches about "seeking the truth"?

____

____

____

____

**Note: You now know what the Bible teaches about seeking truth based on your own discovery. Your belief is grounded in your own research not in what someone else told you, CONGRATULATIONS!*

2. What claims does the Bible make about Jesus? You can look to his birth, baptism, resurrection. *(Read all of the provided scripture before determining which passages answer this question)*

Matthew 1:18-25, Isaiah 11:1-10, Matthew 3:13-17, Isaiah 7:14, Jeremiah 23:5, Micah 5:2, Psalm 91: 10-12, Zechariah 9:9, John 11:25-26, Luke 24:2-3, Peter 1:3-4

Scripture: ____________________________

Paraphrase (In your own words) ____

____

____

Please explain what this scripture means to you. _______________________________________

____

____

____

Scripture: ____________________________

Paraphrase (In your own words) ____

____

____

Please explain what this scripture means to you. _______________________________________

____

____

____

Scripture: ____________________________

Paraphrase (In your own words) ____

Please explain what this scripture means to you.

Based on the scripture you just found in the Bible and your own interpretation, what claims does the Bible make about Jesus?

3. What does the Bible teach about sin and seeking forgiveness?
(Read all of the provided scripture before determining which passages answer this question)

John 11:25-26, Matthew 6:14-15, Psalm 103:12, Luke 24:2-3, 1 John 1:9, Romans 3:23, Romans 6:23, Matthew 26:28, Romans 12:1, Ephesians 2:8-10, Matthew 5:23-24, John 3:16

Scripture:

Paraphrase (In your own words)

____

____

Please explain what this scripture means to you. ______________________________

____

____

____

Scripture: ____________________

Paraphrase (In your own words) ______________________________________

____

____

Please explain what this scripture means to you. ______________________________

____

____

____

Scripture: ____________________

Paraphrase (In your own words) ______________________________________

____

____

Please explain what this scripture means to you. ______________________________

____

____

____

Based on the scripture you just found in the Bible and your own interpretation, what claims does the Bible make about sin and forgiveness?

____

____

____

____

4. What does the Bible teach about salvation?

(Read all of the provided scripture before determining which passages answer this question)

Jeremiah 23:5, Luke 24:2-3, Romans 10:9-10, 1 John 5:11-12, Romans 5:8, Ephesians 2:8-9, Matthew 5:43-48, Daniel 6:23

Scripture: ____________________

Paraphrase (In your own words) ______________________________

____

____

Please explain what this scripture means to you. ____________________

____

____

____

Scripture: ____________________

Paraphrase (In your own words) ______________________________

____

____

Please explain what this scripture means to you. ____

____

____

____

Scripture: ______________________________

Paraphrase (In your own words) ____

____

____

Please explain what this scripture means to you. ____

____

____

____

Based on the scripture you just found in the Bible and your own interpretation, what claims does the Bible make about salvation?

____

____

____

____

____

____

____

What have you learned from this exercise? ______________________________________

____

____

____

____

____

____

____

____

How will you apply what you've learned in this exercise to your life (be specific)? ___________

____

____

____

____

____

____

____

____

SECTION 7

Exercise: Spiritual Relationships

When Jesus was asked "what is the most important command of all?" He responded by saying "Love God with all your heart, soul, strength and mind." The next greatest command is to love your neighbor as much as yourself.

How does God define love? Read the following scripture.

1 Corinthians 13

If I speak in the tongues of men and of angels, but have not love, I am a noisy gong or a clanging
cymbal. 2 And if I have prophetic powers, and understand all mysteries and all knowledge, and if
I have all faith, so as to remove mountains, but have not love, I am nothing. 3 If I give away all I
have, and if I deliver up my body to be burned, but have not love, I gain nothing.

4 Love is patient and kind; love does not envy or boast; it is not arrogant 5 or rude. It does not
insist on its own way; it is not irritable or resentful; 6 it does not rejoice at wrongdoing,
but rejoices with the truth. 7 Love bears all things, believes all things, hopes all things, endures
all things.

8 Love never ends. As for prophecies, they will pass away; as for tongues, they will cease; as for
knowledge, it will pass away. 9 For we know in part and we prophesy in part, 10 but when the
perfect comes, the partial will pass away. 11 When I was a child, I spoke like a child, I thought
like a child, I reasoned like a child. When I became a man, I gave up childish ways. 12 For now we
see in a mirror dimly, but then face to face. Now I know in part; then I shall know fully, even as I
have been fully known.

13 So now faith, hope, and love abide, these three; but the greatest of these is love.

What does this Scripture mean to you?

____

____

____

____

List five characteristics of love (according to the passage)

____

____

____

____

____

"HAPPINESS IS ONLY REAL WHEN SHARED"

— Jon Krakauer, Into the Wild

Relationships

The Bible speaks to the importance of relationships not just on a personal level, but on a spiritual level as well. Answer the following questions to determine what the Bible teaches about relationships with others and your relationship with God.

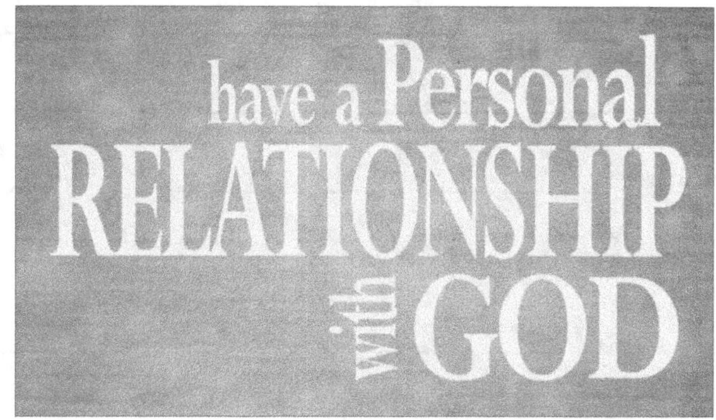

1. What does the Bible teach about **relationships** with others?
(Read all of the provided scripture before determining which passages answer this question)

John 1:1, John 15:13, Ephesians 6:12, Proverbs 17:17, Proverbs 27:17, Galatians 6:2, Genesis 2:18, John 13:34-35, 1 Thessalonians 5:11, 1John 4:4,

Scripture: ______________________________

Paraphrase (In your own words) ____

____

____

Please explain what this scripture means to you. ____________________________________

____

____

____

Scripture: ______________________________

Paraphrase (In your own words) ____

____

____

Please explain what this scripture means to you. ______________________________

____

____

Scripture: ____________________

Paraphrase (In your own words) ______________________________

____

____

Please explain what this scripture means to you. ______________________________

____

____

____

Based on the scripture you just found in the Bible and your own interpretation, what does the Bible teach about relationships with others?

____

____

____

____

____

____

____

2. What does the Bible teach about God's relationship with us (His creation)?
(Read all of the provided scripture before determining which passages answer this question)

John 14:6, Hebrews 13:5, John 15:15, John 14:23, 1Corithians 15: 3-8, John 15:15, Ephesians 2:19, Romans 8:15, John 3:16, 2 Timothy 2:18,

Scripture: ____________________________

Paraphrase (In your own words) ____

____

____

Please explain what this scripture means to you. ___________________________________

____

____

____

Scripture: ____________________________

Paraphrase (In your own words) ____

____

____

Please explain what this scripture means to you. ___________________________________

____

____

____

Scripture: ____________________________

Paraphrase (In your own words) ____

____

____

Please explain what this scripture means to you. ________________________________

____

____

____

Based on the scripture you just found in the Bible and your own interpretation, what does the Bible teach about having a God's relationship to his creation?

____

____

____

____

____

____

____

What have you learned from this exercise? ________________________________

____

____

____

____

SECTION 8

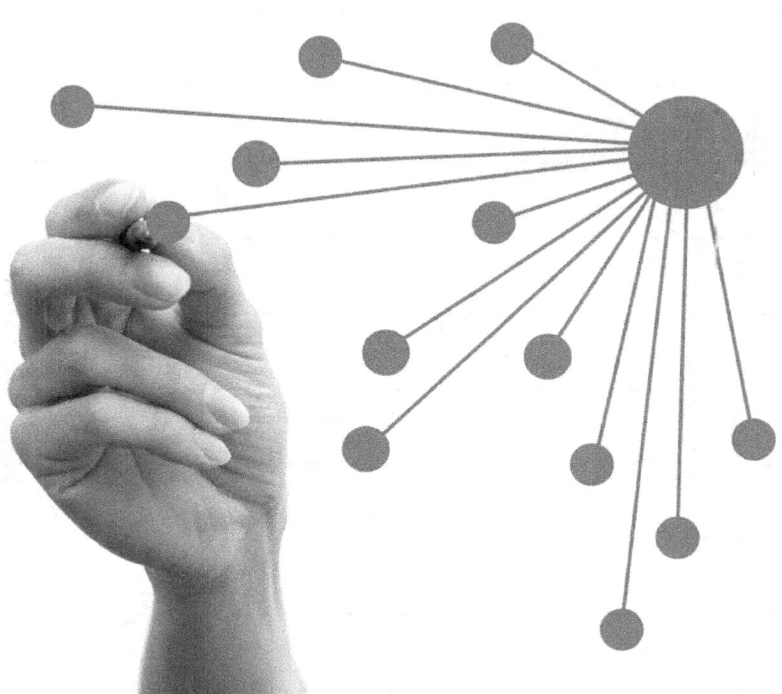

Exercise: Connecting the Dots

During this workshop you have examined your life, spirituality, relationships, and stumbling blocks. By inspecting your life and developing a plan for the future you increase the likelihood of success. This last exercise will focus on connecting the dots. You will be reviewing what you have learned and discussing what you will do with this information.

Note:

During this last session you will also review your Individual Program Plan. Please make sure it is complete including all required signatures.

(Using all the space provided answer the following questions)

1. What do you know now about yourself that you did not know before you began this workshop?

____

____

____

____

____

____

____

____

____

____

____

____

____

____

____

____

____

____

2. What is the importance of relationships to your life? Please explain.

3. What changes (or clarification) in thought or behavior have you noticed in your own spiritual life over the past eight weeks?

HELLO
my name is
CHANGE

4. What goals have you set for yourself in this workshop?

5. How will your goals help you succeed?

6. What are the stumbling blocks you need to watch out for?

7. What will you do when you recognize a stumbling block?

____

____

____

____

____

____

8. What was the most helpful part of this workshop?

____

____

____

____

____

____

9. Was the hardest part of this workshop? Please explain.

____

____

____

____

10. Write a prayer for your future

Conclusion:

John F. Kennedy said, "Change is the law of life. And those who look only to the past or present are certain to miss the future." This workshop wasn't meant to fix mistakes from the past but merely help to prepare for a better future.

It took a lifetime to get where you are now and it will take some time to get to where you want to go. The difference between where you've been and where you want to go is in how you handle those mistakes, hurts and pains when they come along. Never give up, always push forward. Change is often slow but worth the effort. Remember scripture teaches us, "Don't grow weary of doing good, for in due season we will reap, if we do not give up" (Galatians 6:9).

May you continue to grow and discover the hope, peace and strength that can be found in healthy relationships with others and with God. ~Amen

www.ingramcontent.com/pod-product-compliance
Lightning Source LLC
Chambersburg PA
CBHW081404280526
45788CB00009B/2983

9781530472666